Looking at Countries

GREAT BRITAIN

Jillian Powell

FRANKLIN WATTS
LONDON·SYDNEY

First published in 2006 by
Franklin Watts
338 Euston Road
London NW1 3BH

Franklin Watts Australia
Hachette Children's Books
Level 17/207 Kent Street
Sydney NSW 2000

ISBN-10: 0 7496 6479 7
ISBN-13: 978 0 7496 6479 4
Dewey classification: 914.1

Series editor: Sarah Peutrill
Art director: Jonathan Hair
Design: Storeybooks Ltd
Cover design: Peter Scoulding
Picture research: Diana Morris

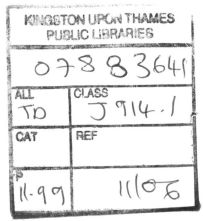

Picture credits: Sheila Attar/Cordaiy Photo. Library/Corbis: 18. Eleanor Bentall/Corbis: 21b. Martin Bond/Photofusion: 12,19t. Bryn Colton/Assignments Photographers/Corbis: 20. Ashley Cooper/Corbis: 10, 17, 21t. Joe Cornish/National Trust Picture Library: 7b. Peter Dench/Corbis: 9t. Adrian Don/Photographers Direct: front cover inset, 16. Robert Estall/Corbis: 9b. Malcolm Fife/zefa/Corbis: 19b. Paul Hardy/Corbis: 1, 27. The Hoberman Collection/Alamy: 23b. Dewitt Jones/Corbis: 11. Gareth Wyn-Jones/Photofusion: 22. Ray Juno/Corbis: 6. Gary Lee/UPPA/Topfoto: 25t. Tim MacMillan/Garden Picture Library/Alamy: 25b. Christine Osborne/Corbis: 13. Robert Paterson/Reuters/Corbis: 24. Derry Robinson/National Trust Picture Library: 7t. Christa Stadtler/Photofusion: 23t. Superbild/A1 Pix: 26b. Sandro Vianni/Corbis: 4b. Patrick Ward/Corbis: 8. Josh Westrick/zefa/Corbis: 26t. Adam Woolfitt/Corbis: front cover main, 14, 15. Every attempt has been made to clear copyright. Should there be any inadvertent omission please apply to the publisher for rectification.

A CIP catalogue record for this book is available from the British Library.

Printed in China

Contents

Where is Great Britain?

Great Britain is an island made up of three countries: England, Scotland and Wales. It is in western Europe.

Northern Ireland

Great Britain

Britain is part of the United Kingdom (UK) with Northern Ireland.

London is the capital city of both England and Great Britain; Edinburgh is the capital of Scotland and Cardiff is the capital of Wales. Britain has many historic buildings including fine houses, castles and cathedrals.

Edinburgh Castle is one of Britain's most visited monuments.

Use this map to find the places mentioned in this book.

GREAT BRITAIN

Orkney Islands

Outer Hebrides

SCOTLAND

Dornie

Grampians

Shetland Islands

ATLANTIC OCEAN

EDINBURGH

Glasgow

NORTH SEA

Hebrides

Inner

NORTHERN IRELAND

Newcastle

Durham

Robin Hood's Bay

Pennines

Cumbria

Yorkshire

REPUBLIC OF IRELAND

Isle of Man

Burnley

Leeds

IRISH SEA

Manchester

Grimsby

Sheffield

ENGLAND

Cambrian

WALES

Birmingham

Norwich

East Anglia

NETHERLANDS

CARDIFF

Thames

LONDON

Southend-on-Sea

BELGIUM

Rhossili Bay

Cotswolds

South Downs

Channel Tunnel

Cornwall

ENGLISH CHANNEL

Isles of Scilly

Mousehole

FRANCE

Channel Islands

Great Britain has a coastline along the Atlantic Ocean in the west, and the North Sea in the east. The Irish Sea lies between Ireland and Great Britain. The English Channel is between France and Great Britain.

Did you know?

Britain is joined to France by a tunnel under the English Channel.

5

The landscape

Great Britain has many sorts of landscape. The highest mountains are in Scotland, northern England and Wales. In the north, there are also lakes and high moors where sheep graze.

Did you know?

Wales is the most important place in Europe for sheep farming.

Eilean Donan castle is on the west coast of Scotland, near the village of Dornie. It is on a small island at the meeting point of three lochs – the Scottish word for lakes.

Grasses and wildflowers grow on the Sussex Downs.

Most land suitable for growing crops is in the middle and south, where there are gentle hills. In the far south are the hilly grasslands of the Downs.

The coastline also changes, from the rugged rocky cliffs on the west, to the wide sandy beaches of East Anglia.

Robin Hood's Bay in north-east England is famous for the rock pools on its beach.

Weather and seasons

Great Britain has a temperate climate, with warm summers and cool winters. Scotland and the north have the coldest winters, with snow on the mountains and hills.

Winter snow falls most often on higher ground like the North York Moors in Yorkshire.

Holidaymakers stay on the beach even on a rainy summer's day at Southend-on-Sea in the south-east.

Heavy rain can sometimes make rivers flood in winter. There can be drought in warm summer months, although it usually rains all year round.

The south is the sunniest part of the country. In the south-west and the Isles of Scilly, the warm Gulf Stream from the Atlantic Ocean brings mild winters, allowing even sub-tropical plants to grow.

Did you know?

The Lake District in Cumbria in the north is England's wettest area.

Summer sunshine bathes the golden sands of Rhossili Bay, Gower, Wales.

British people

This food store in Burnley in the north is in an area with a large Asian community.

People have lived, and moved to live, in Great Britain for thousands of years. In the last 100 years people have moved to Britain from lots of different places including India, Pakistan, Africa, the Caribbean and China. Many groups have settled in big cities such as London, Birmingham and Manchester.

Did you know?

The Notting Hill Carnival in London celebrates Caribbean culture.

This man is showing off two symbols of Scotland, Highland cattle and the kilt, the national dress of Scotland.

The main religion in Britain is Christianity. Most Christians belong to the Protestant Church of England or Scotland but there are also many Roman Catholics. There are large communities of Muslims, Hindus, Sikhs and Jews living in Britain as well.

English is the main language, although it is spoken in many different accents and dialects. Welsh, Gaelic, Punjabi, Hindi and Urdu are also spoken.

Family and school

Family life is important in Britain. Most children live with their families. There are lots of different types of family. Many children live with just their mum or dad or with step-families.

Places like this sandy 'beach' in the middle of a city give city families a chance to have a fun day out.

Children wearing their school uniform sing at morning assembly at a primary school in London.

Most children start school when they are five years old. Many start earlier, at nurseries, or go to childminders, if both parents are working.

The school day usually starts at 9 am and finishes at 3.30 pm. Children whose parents are working may go on to after-school clubs where they can do sports and other activities.

Did you know?

In parts of Wales, children have their school lessons in the Welsh language.

Country

Only one in ten people in Britain live in the country. Many people have moved into towns and cities to find work, as there are more jobs there.

About three-quarters of the countryside is farmland. Some farmers have also started new businesses, such as farm shops and farm holidays. They sometimes use farm buildings for local crafts and other industries.

A traditional cream tea, of scones and bread rolls with cream and jam, served in the garden of a farm tea-shop.

Mousehole is a typical fishing village in Cornwall. Many people have holiday homes there.

Most country people live in villages or market towns which have a church, small shops and a pub. There may be out-of-town superstores nearby for shopping. Some houses have become second homes or holiday homes for people living in cities.

Did you know?

Most of Britain was once covered in forest and woodland.

City

Most people in Britain live in towns or cities. London, the capital, is the largest city in Britain. Over seven million people live there. Birmingham, Leeds and Glasgow are the next largest cities.

The Quayside and Millennium Bridge are part of the recent waterfront development of Newcastle.

Many cities such as Durham and Norwich have old centres with a cathedral, churches, a castle and old houses. Some cities have had older areas redeveloped recently, particularly areas by rivers and canals.

Over one million people travel into London by underground trains, called 'the tube' every day.

Did you know?

Birmingham has more canals than Venice, Italy.

Traffic is a problem on Britain's busy roads and in city centres. In London and Glasgow, most people travel by underground trains. Birmingham, Manchester and Sheffield have trams as well as buses for public transport.

British homes

Britain has many kinds of homes. In the country, there are many old houses and cottages. They are built from stone or have timber frames with thatched or tiled roofs. New houses on the edge of villages or towns are often built in traditional styles.

Many old cottages like this one in the Cotswolds are over 500 years old.

The largest houses in Britain are historic stately homes. Many are now open to the public as tourist attractions.

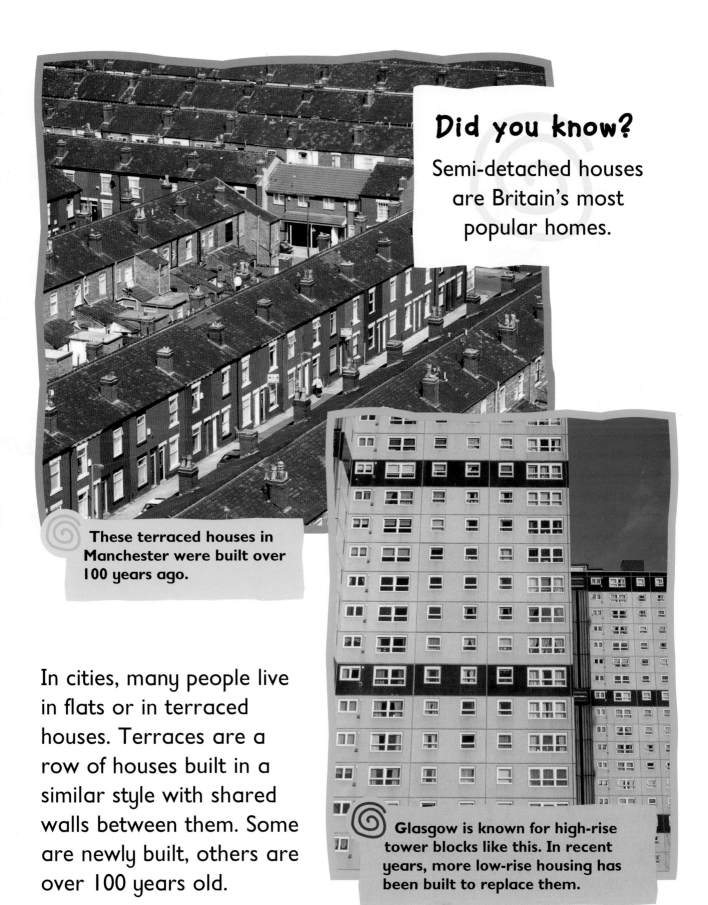

Did you know?

Semi-detached houses are Britain's most popular homes.

These terraced houses in Manchester were built over 100 years ago.

In cities, many people live in flats or in terraced houses. Terraces are a row of houses built in a similar style with shared walls between them. Some are newly built, others are over 100 years old.

Glasgow is known for high-rise tower blocks like this. In recent years, more low-rise housing has been built to replace them.

Food

Many British people shop in supermarkets for their food, but there are also market squares or street markets in most towns and cities.

There has been an open-air market in Norwich, Norfolk, for about 800 years.

Traditional British dishes include roast beef with potatoes and vegetables, and cooked breakfast of bacon and eggs.

Did you know?

Britain's most popular dish is curry. This is a spicy dish of meat or vegetables, which comes from Indian cooking.

This man is selling local cheeses from a stall at a country fair.

Some dishes, such as Yorkshire pudding and Cornish pasties, came from particular areas but are eaten throughout Britain. Haggis, traditionally made from a mixture of meat and oats cooked in a sheep's stomach, is the national dish of Scotland. There are also many British cheeses, such as Cheddar and Wensleydale.

Fish and chips is the traditional takeaway food in Britain, but there are many other fast foods such as fried chicken and burgers. Chinese, Indian and Italian foods are also popular.

Fish and chips wrapped in paper is a popular takeaway meal.

At work

The main industries in Britain include machine tools, food processing, tourism and clothing. There are also jobs in the aircraft industry and assembling cars.

Did you know?

Tourism is one of Britain's biggest industries, providing over two million jobs.

These men are preparing fish at a factory in Grimsby on the north-east coast.

This maths teacher is helping students. Teaching is one of the most popular jobs for workers in Great Britain.

Service industries such as banking and insurance have grown fast in Britain. In towns and cities, many people work in offices, or in shops, schools or hospitals.

These police officers are on duty at London's Buckingham Palace.

Having fun

Football, cricket and rugby are all popular sports in Britain. During the football season, many families enjoy going to watch their local team play. Big sports events include the Wimbledon tennis tournament and the Football Association (FA) Cup.

Did you know?

Watching television is Britain's most popular leisure activity.

Celtic fans cheer their team at a match against rival Rangers in the Scottish Premier League.

Christmas and Easter are important Christian festivals when people celebrate by going to church and gathering for special meals with their family. Hindu festivals such as Holi and Divali, and Muslim festivals such as Id-ul-Fitr, are also celebrated.

Pantomimes are traditional Christmas shows with song and dance, based on fairytale stories and characters.

Many other events such as country fêtes and fairs are held around the country during the warmer summer months.

Many people in Britain enjoy gardening. These people are at the Chelsea flower show, which is held every year in London.

Britain: the facts

• Great Britain, as part of the UK, is a member of the European Union. The Queen is the head of state and the Prime Minister leads the government.

• Britain has over 100 regions called counties and over 600 constituencies. Each constituency has its own Member of Parliament (MP) chosen by people living there.

The British currency is the pound. Every note and coin has a picture of the Queen on it.

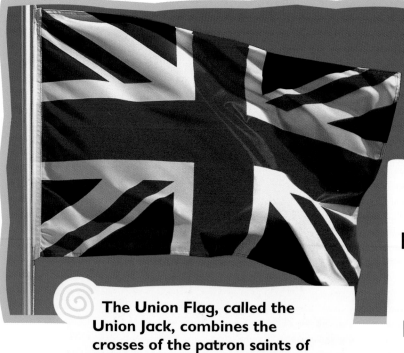

The Union Flag, called the Union Jack, combines the crosses of the patron saints of England, Ireland and Scotland.

Did you know?

Big Ben is the name of the bell inside the clock tower of the Houses of Parliament.

The London Eye (a giant observation wheel) is a new landmark on the River Thames.

• About 59 million people live in Great Britain. Britain, as part of the UK, also has a number of overseas dependencies including the Channel Islands, Bermuda (an island in the Atlantic Ocean, off the coast of the USA) and Gibraltar (next to the south coast of Spain). The Commonwealth of Nations is a group of independent overseas countries that were once ruled by Britain.

• London, Britain's capital, has many grand old buildings, parks, museums and art galleries as well as new landmarks such as the Millennium Bridge and the London Eye.

Glossary

Accents the way you say a word or speak generally.

Canal a waterway made for boats to transport goods.

Constituencies districts that have Members of Parliament to represent them.

Cornish pasty a type of pie that comes from Cornwall. It has a pastry case and is filled with meat and vegetables.

Dependencies land or countries ruled by another country.

Dialects different ways of speaking a language.

Downs areas of rolling, mainly treeless, grassy land.

Drought a long period of time with little or no rain.

European Union a group of European countries that have joined together to share trade, laws and, if they choose to, a single currency (the Euro).

Gulf Stream a warm current in the North Atlantic Ocean.

Head of state the person who represents a country.

Member of Parliament someone who is elected by the people in their constituency to represent them in Parliament.

Moors open, high land.

Parliament the place where laws are made.

Patron saint a person who is believed to represent a country in heaven.

Redevelop to develop land in a different way.

Rock pool a pool of water, often full of animal and plant life, that is left on a beach when the sea goes out.

Scone a soft cake usually made from flour, butter and milk.

Semi-detatched a pair of houses built with a shared wall between them.

Service industry an industry that provides a service, e.g. banking, insurance.

Sub-tropical describes the climate or plants near the Tropics, or plants that are similar that grow elsewhere.

Temperate never very hot or very cold.

Yorkshire pudding a food made from a batter of flour, milk and eggs, which is usually eaten with a main course.

Find out more

www.woodlands-junior.kent.sch.uk/geography/Britain.html
An award-winning school website packed with information on topics including food, culture and sport with interactive games.

www.britainusa.com/4kids
The children's section of a website for the British Embassy in the USA, with topics including sport, history, books and fashion.

www.timeforkids.com/TFK/hh/goplaces [Click England]
A guide to England with famous sites, a history timeline and a factfile.

Note to parents and teachers: Every effort has been made by the Publishers to ensure that these websites are suitable for children, that they are of the highest educational value, and that they contain no inappropriate or offensive material. However, because of the nature of the Internet, it is impossible to guarantee that the contents of these sites will not be altered. We strongly advise that Internet access is supervised by a responsible adult.

Gaelic and Welsh

Scottish Gaelic is spoken by about 66,000 people, mainly in the west and north-west of Scotland.

Gaelic	English	Say ...
Gabh mo lethsgeul	Excuse me	ga muh lyesh-kyal
Madainn mhath	Good morning	matiny vah
Mas e ur toil e	Please	ma-sheh ur tol eh
Tapadh leibh	Thank you	ta-puh laiv
Thugainn	Let's go	hu-kiny
Tha mi duilich	I'm sorry	ha mee doo-leech

Welsh is spoken by over 500,000 people. It is taught in Welsh schools and there is also a Welsh television channel.

Welsh	English	Say ...
Diolch	Thank you	dee-olkh
Esgusodwch fi	Excuse me	ess-gi-so-dookh vee
Hwyl fawr	Goodbye	hool-ell vowrr
Mae'n ddrwg gyda fi	Sorry	main thrroog guh-da vee
Os gwelwch yn dda	Please	os gwel-ookh uhn thah
Sut mae	Hello	shoo mai

My map of Great Britain

Trace this map, colour it in and use the map on
page 5 to write the names of the main places.

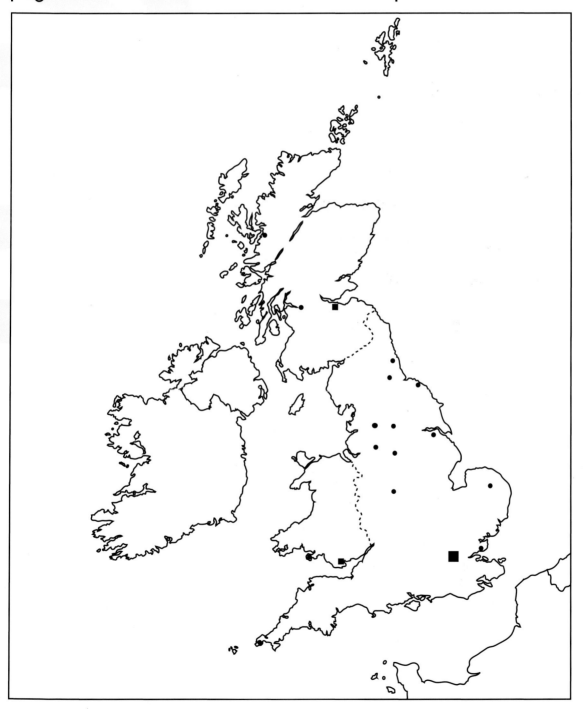

Index